Clouds of Winter

Ritu Oraon

BookLeaf Publishing

India | USA | UK

Presentation by *BookLeaf Publishing*

Web: www.bookleafpub.com

E-mail: info@bookleafpub.com

ISBN: 9789363311947

First edition 2024

This book of poems is dedicated to my wonderful kids and my loving husband, whose unwavering support, boundless patience, and endless encouragement have been the foundation upon which these words were built. This collection is a testament to the love and inspiration you provide, and I hope these poems reflect the warmth and happiness you bring into my world. Thank you for being my constant support, which is inevitable in publishing this collection.

ACKNOWLEDGEMENT

I would like to express my deepest gratitude to all those who have supported me throughout the creation of this book of poems. To my family and friends, your unwavering encouragement and understanding have been invaluable. To my mentors and teachers, your guidance and wisdom have shaped my craft and inspired my voice. A special thank you to my husband and children for their boundless patience and love, which have been my greatest source of strength. I am also grateful to my readers, whose appreciation for poetry motivates me to continue writing. This book is a reflection of all the love, support, and inspiration I have received, and I am profoundly thankful for each and every one of you.

PREFACE

In the hustle and bustle of our daily lives, poetry offers a moment of stillness, a chance to pause and reflect. This collection of poems is born from such moments—when the world slows down and emotions rise to the surface, demanding to be expressed. Through these verses, I aim to capture the essence of the human experience: the joys, sorrows, dreams, and reflections that shape our lives. Each poem is a journey, an exploration of the heart and mind, inspired by the beauty and complexity of our existence.

This book is a culmination of years of introspection, observation, and the desire to connect with others through words. The poems within these pages are a mosaic of my thoughts and feelings, woven together to form a tapestry of experiences that I hope will resonate with you. Whether you find solace, inspiration, or a sense of shared understanding, my wish is that these poems touch your soul and offer a glimpse into the universal truths that bind us all.

As you embark on this poetic journey, I invite you to open your heart and mind, to savor each word, and to find your own meanings within these lines. Poetry is a mirror, reflecting not only the poet's world but also the reader's inner landscape. May this collection serve as a companion in your own moments of stillness and contemplation.

You are In Love

When you feel light, energetic, excited
When every cell of the body feels alive

When you feel current in your body
From the stomach to the tip of fingers

From head to toe,
Everything gets electrified

When heartbeat gets fastened,
And breathing gets hard,

When every cell of your body
Is happy and feeling light

As if floating in the air
And can go anywhere

When your mind is occupied
By the thoughts of him

And feels the urge to talk...
Every day, every moment

Then a sudden thought pops up
Ohh! Maybe you are in Love

I know you from many Births

Your existence is enough for me to live
No matter how hard
I try not to think about you
You are always on my mind

This feeling for you
is burning me from inside
I am sinking
In this feeling of heaviness
Craving for your presence

For your touch
For deeper connection
your slight touch
electrified my entire sense of me
and bring my spirit alive

My Spirit is screaming loud
for your companionship
It feels as if you are my soul family
And I know you from many births

Reciprocal Feeling

It's getting hard and suffocating
to not communicate
I am only thinking of myself
my spirit, my body
I think every cell of my body
Craves you, your touch

Although I have never told you,
How do I feel
My eyes betray every time
Whenever I see you

I think it's mutual and reciprocal feeling
I know you also feel the same
I can sense it,
but because of earthy boundaries
You are resisting, and so do I

Timeless love

I don't understand
what is this feeling

When I am not with you
It felt eons to pass.

When I am with you
time freezes

When you come to me
My heart's pulsating fast

When you are with me
My breathing stops

Feeling as if this continues
My heart is going to explode

All I Want

All I want is
To know the quantity of energy
I perceive from your heart

All I want is
To know why my heart bleeds
When you ignore me

All I want is
To understand why
My spirit wants you
To get entangled with you

All I want is
To understand whether
I am real or
Some imagination
In the minds of God

All I want is
To understand why do
Humans have emotions

All I want is
To understand my existence
In this Multiverse

All I want is
To understand everything
And everything's everything

Turbulence Emotions

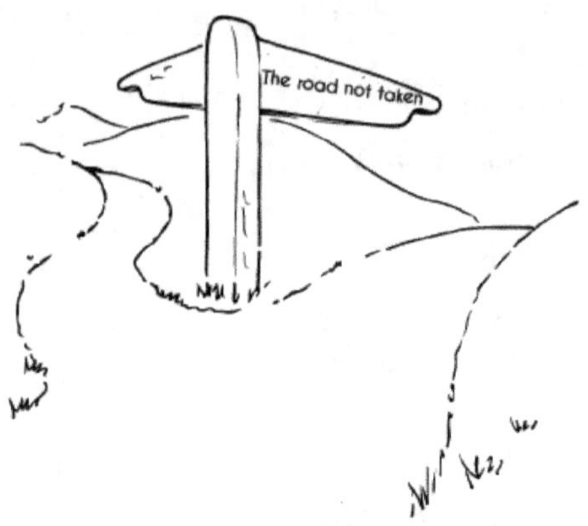

I cannot lose Myself
So, I resisted

The more I resisted
The more it existed

To calm my fluttering
I reveal my feeling

Never knew I am not your type
And got rejected

It was embarrassing
But still, I am addicted

I hate this feeling
But still Its hovering

My heart skips a beat
Whenever our eyes meet

Ohh!!!
I never was this helpless

Righteous Feeling

I hate this feeling
It feels so right

I feel some invisible force
pulling me
tremendously towards you

I feel powerless
In front of this
invisible, forceful attraction

Not able to hold
And control myself

The pull is so strong
That every cell of my body

Gets activated
And demand of you

To hug you, to kiss you
To feel you, to love you

So, I am afraid of myself
I may lose control of me

I should feel guilty
Why it feels so Right

Free Birds

I love you and you love me
We travel the journey of life together

But I forget that to travel together
Constantly I am forcing you to be together

I bounded myself for your love
Limiting you to other
So that I become your priority

Later finding, I am not connected
Neither by you Nor by myself

Your soul wants freedom from me
Wondering what I have done gone wrong

Limiting our boundaries
I become someone else
Our love becomes suffocating

Our soul wants to break boundaries
Even though it's tough and hard
We separated

Now we are free birds
It feels good to travel together
With no boundaries and Limitations

Mother's Guilt

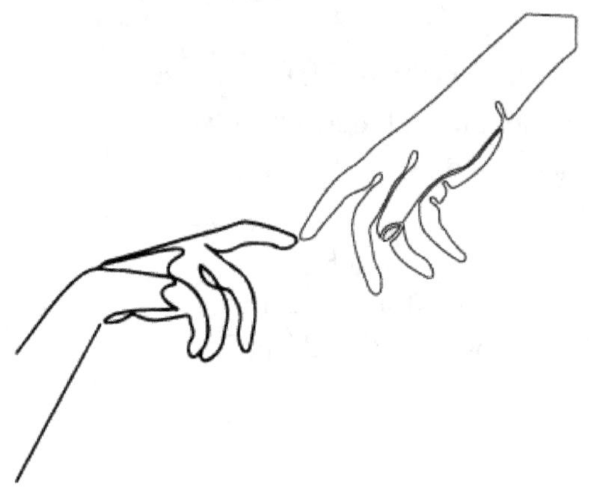

It's hard and difficult
Excruciating pain in my heart

Tears in my eyes
Watching you cry

Filled with guilt
Not able to provide

The love you required
Leaving you alone

In the house
With the maid

Days and Nights out
Moving to the field

Choosing my job
Its so hard

Crying my heart loud
Filled with anxiety

Cannot bear the pain
Actually it's guilt

Without me
How you will survive

My Shona, My Bittu
My Love, My son

Waiting for you to grow

Girl, You hold power
When you work

When you contribute
When you give output

Girl, people will respect you
A sense of worthiness

When money is in your Bank account
When you are able to help people

Remember
When you help

The universe will help you
Three times more, what you desire

So, learn some skills
Teach it to others

Study hard, Be the worthy
Work on yourself
World is waiting for you

You are about to Shine

You have grown your wings
You just need to fly

You have to dream big
Question everything why

Make effort each day
Towards achieving your dream

Take action, Step by step
And receiving step by step

You have grown your wings
Girl, you are about to shine

Soaked into Rain

Water dripping from my body
Unwary of my white kurti

Being transparent
My specs being blurry

Moving like blindly
From last 45 minutes

Pitter Patter, Tip tip
Soaked into the rain

From head to toe
Feeling cold, Shivering
In the month of April

My scooty stops
In the middle of nowhere

No one is on the Road
With the fear in heart

My heart pulsating fast
Whom to call for help

Pitter Patter, Tip Tip
Soaked into the rain

Thank you Universe

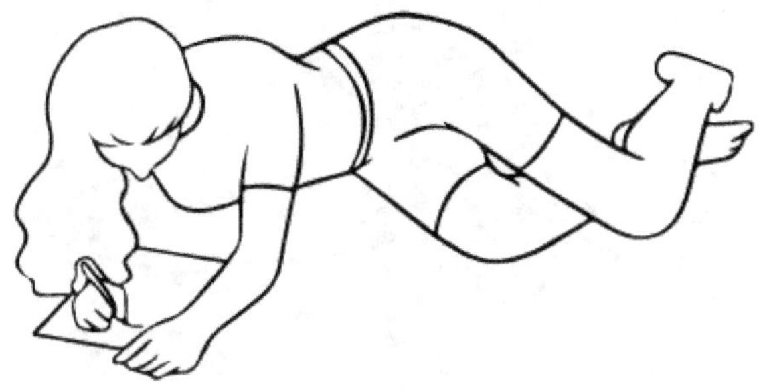

Thank you, universe,
For the love, affection, and care

For being a part of my life
For letting me realize

The anxious feeling of Love
Pain & Breathlessness

Teaching how to ignore
And not to care

How to ignore
And not to care

Intention of people
Nasty gossips, toxic people
Maligning pure heart

How we came on the Earth

I want to go beyond boundaries
Moving in the Jungle
Feeling mountains

Touch the rock
Feel their pain

From billions of years
They trapped beneath
The ground.

I want to know them
I want to feel them

Just Curious
How they evolve

How Himalayas grow so big
How Rivers trace their paths
How we came on this earth

Innocent Girl

Innocent girl with dreams to fly
I must add values in Life

Clipped by societal expectations
I want to document my Life

Every moment, every thought
I want to become free

To break boundaries
I have to fly high

But This world operates differently
In shades, In various layers

Masked People, far from truth
Don't trust, you will die

Your perception of Me

Your perception of me
doesn't define me

You think I am weak,
Because I show you my vulnerability

You think I cannot do for myself
Because I have done only for you

I definitely will show the world
What can I do and can't do

The fire in me is burning
To prove myself

Its enough
I am ready

To be courageous
And fight for me

To prove myself
I will go beyond boundaries

I will touch the sky
Bring the world into my hand

I will show the world
Not the way you want me to
But with Kindness and Love

I want to Thank Me

I want to thank me
For being me all the time

I want to thank me
For believing in myself

I want to thank me
For doing all the hard work

I want to thank me
For never quitting

I want to thank me
For being a giver
Giving more than average

I want to thank me
To bring great wealth
To bring endless happiness
To bring abundant joy
By being me all the time

I am the one
Turning my pain into power
Fear into Focus
Difficulties into blessings
Hardships into opportunities

First Time Mother

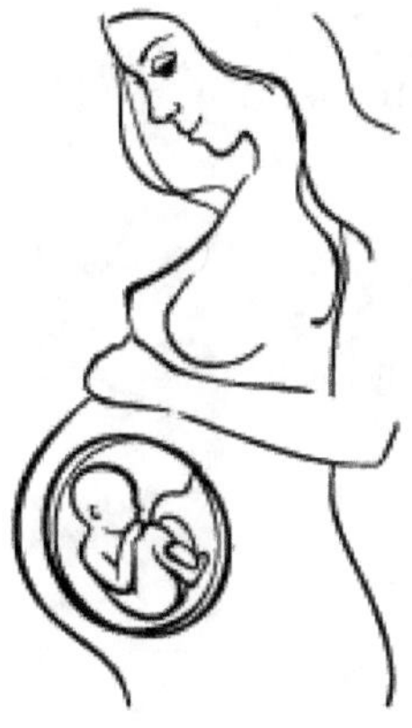

It is a struggle,
to be a first-time mother

Crying, crying, every night
Every day, unable to settle

12:00 am, sleep in the eyes
Baby started crying,
Continuously, Inconsolably

One hour pass
Two hours pass
Colicky baby,

Nobody told what is colic
To a new mother

Unable to understand
how to relieve the pain
of my infant

My heart is breaking
Watching him in Pain

Working Mother

In the dawn's first light, she starts her day,
A working mother, finding her way.

With a five-year-old in tow, so bright,
She juggles work with all her might.

A bag in one hand, a child's toy in the other,
She's a manager, a mentor, and a loving mother.

Meetings to attend, deadlines to meet,
While tiny feet patter and toys clutter her seat.

Emails to answer, phone calls to make,
A snack for her child, a quick coffee break.

Her toddler's laughter, a sweet, joyful sound,
In the chaos, a moment of calm is found.

Colleagues whisper, some with a smile,
Admiring her strength, her unending style.

But doubts creep in–am I doing enough?
Balancing these worlds is undoubtedly tough.

At times, frustration shadows her grace,
As she wipes chocolate smudges from her face.

Yet in her heart, she knows it's true,
She's setting an example in all that she'll do.

For her child sees a mother so strong,
Teaching resilience all day long.

And though the path is hard to tread,
She carries on with dreams ahead.

With love and patience, she'll always show,
That in both work and home, she'll grow.

In every struggle, she finds her might,
A working mother, shining so bright.

Mother's worry

In Agartala, I wake each day,
With hopes that in my heart do sway.

The thought of Ranchi, fresh and bright,
A future glowing in the light.

An infant's coo, a toddler's cheer,
Amidst my joy, there's hidden fear.

Will I be granted that transfer call,
Or must I stay, here after all?

Each morning brings a heavy sigh,
As dreams of Ranchi flutter by.

Uncertainty wraps me tight,
In whispers of the silent night.

The fear of moving, kids in tow,
To places new where I don't know.

Yet staying here, a path unclear,
With worries that refuse to disappear.

In Ranchi, will I find a place,
Where tiny feet can grow in grace?

Will we adapt, will we belong,
Or will the journey prove too long?

With infant cries and toddler's needs,
I wonder where this path will lead.

A mother's heart, so full of care,
Balancing dreams with a silent prayer.

Each passing day, the tension grows,
As winds of change and doubt still blow.

But deep inside, I hold on tight,
To visions of a hopeful light.

Whether the answer's yes or no,
We'll find our way, we'll learn and grow.

For in this heart, strength does reside,
With my children always by my side.

To Ranchi's call, I yearn to heed,
A place where dreams and lives can lead.